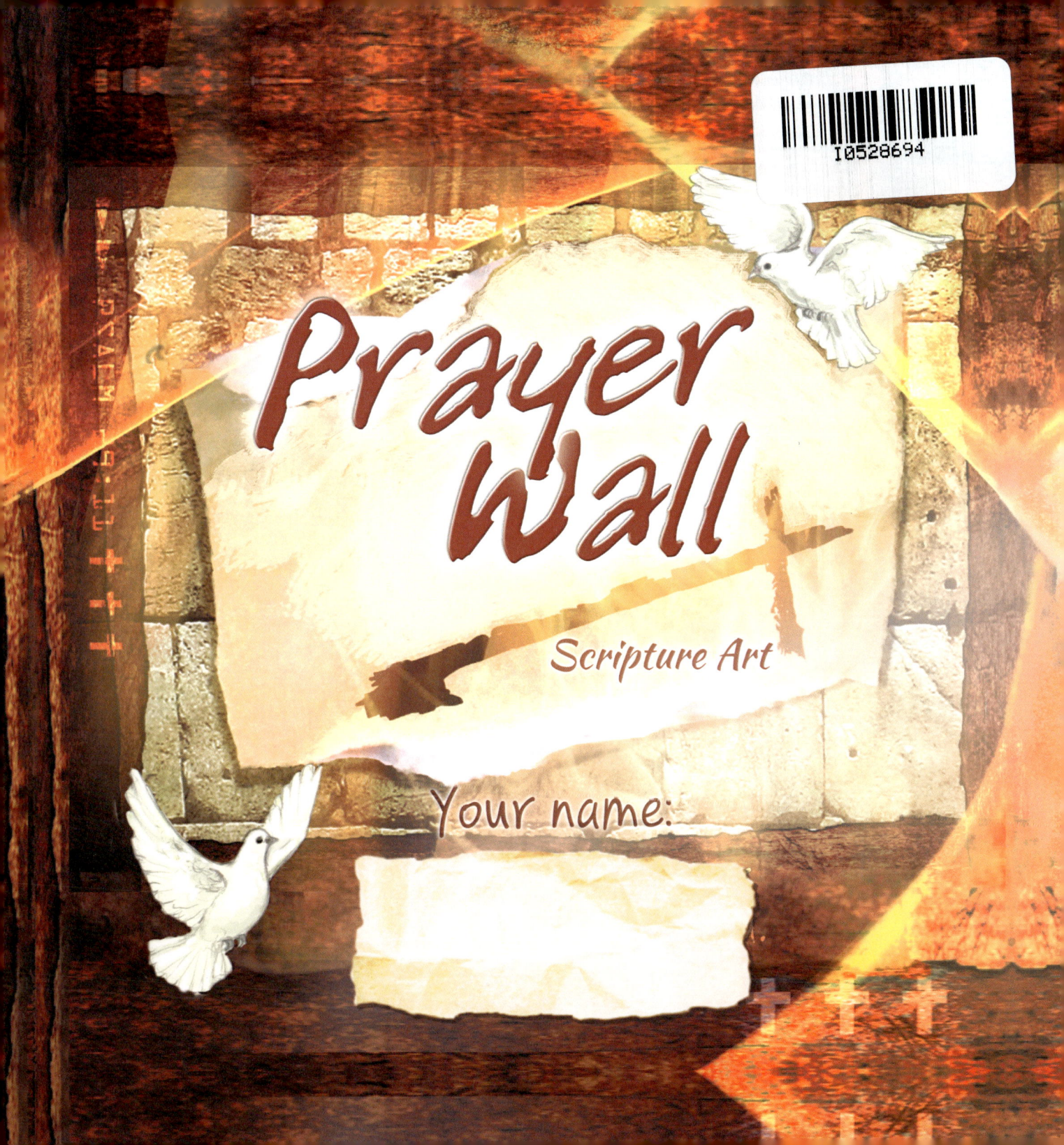

Prayer Wall

Scripture Art

Your name:

peace shall bruise Satan
...rtly. The grace of our
...be with you. Amen.

FOR THE PEA...
SHALL PROSPER...LOVE THE...
WITHIN THY WALLS AND...
...SPERITY WITHIN THY PALACES.
...BRETHREN AND COMPANIONS SAKES
...NOW SAY PEACE BE WITHIN THEE
...EM 122:6-8 KJV

Therefore being justified by faith,
have peace with God through our
Jesus Christ   Romans 5:1 KJV

peace shall bruise Satan
ortly. The grace of our
t be with you. Amen.
JV

FOR THE PEA
SHALL PROSPER LOVE
WITHIN THY WALLS AND
OSPERTLY WITHIN THY PALACES
BRETHREN IONS SAKES
LL NOW SAY PE WITHIN TREE
EM 122:6-8 KJV

Therefore being justified by faith
have peace with God through ou
Jesus Christ   Romans 5:1 KJV

peace shall bruise Satan
ortly. The grace of our
be with you. Amen.
V

FOR THE PEA
SHALL PROSPER LOVE THEE
WITHIN THY WALLS AND
SPERITY WITHIN THY PALACES
BRETHREN AND COMPANIONS SAKES
LL NOW SAY PEACE BE WITHIN THEE
M 122:6-8 KJV

Therefore being justified by faith,
have peace with God through our
Jesus Christ   Romans 5:1 KJV

PRAYER WALL

Published in 2024
by Dawnlight Publishing

ISBN 978-1-99-117680-6 (hardcover)

ISBN 978-1-99-117688-2 (paperback)

Peace Wall artwork designed by Mike Burrows Graphics.
Book layout and illustrations by Mary Marinan.
Text , artwork and creative book concept copyright © Dawnlight Publishing 2024.

Scripture quotations from the King James Version and American Standard Version ~
public domain use.

A catalogue record for this book is available from the National Library of New Zealand

Scripture Art Books

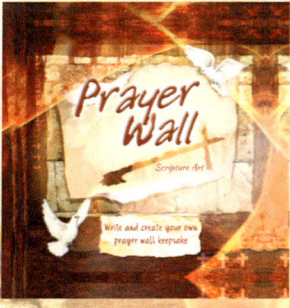

www.ingramcontent.com/pod-product-compliance
Lightning Source LLC
Chambersburg PA
CBRC090834120626
46547CB00009B/679